A Hole in the Boat

Written by Adi Zelichov Relevy

Illustrated by Shiraz Fuman

A Hole in the Boat

Adi Zelichov Relevy

Illustrations: Shiraz Fuman

Translator: Shira Atik
This book was created as an initiative of PJ Library's affiliate in Israel,
Sifriyat Pijama, in cooperation with Yediot Books.

Editor of children's and young adult books: Rinat Primo
Design: Michael Golan
Language and punctuation editor: Sigal Gefen
Charts, printing and binding: Meiri Press

Miskal - Yedioth Ahronoth Books and Chemed Books | P.O.B. 445,
Rishon LeZion 7510302, Israel
E-mail: info@ybook.co.il

Printed in China
042031.3K1/B1049/A6

To Lior, Ilai, Alma and Yali, my loved ones,
for being both anchor and sea breeze.

Adi

For Ayelet, Yehuda, Sharon and Shahar,
whom I would take to a desert island in
a heartbeat.

Shiraz

A Hole in the Boat

~~~

Written by Adi Zelichov Relevy
Illustrated by Shiraz Fuman

Yedioth Ahronoth • Chemed Books

This is no ordinary story. It's thousands of years old, but it's also new. You see, ancient stories in the Torah – the first five books of the Bible – left the readers with lots of questions. And because people are curious and like details, rabbis through the centuries imagined new stories that helped explain what was going on in the old ones. This made the original stories more interesting to hear or read and understand. In Hebrew, a story like that is called a *midrash.*

So here's a question from the Torah: "When one person does wrong, will You [God] be angry with the whole community?"* In other words, should everyone be punished because of what one person does? Almost two thousand years ago, a famous rabbi named Shimon bar Yochai wrote a midrash that helped explain this passage: "Some people were on a ship. One of them took a drill and started drilling through the floorboards. The others said to him: What are you doing?! He replied: What do you care? Aren't I drilling under my own space? They said to him: But the water will rise and flood all of us..."**

A Hole in the Boat is a version of this midrash (and much more fun to read!). As you'll see, one character in the book does pretty much what he chooses. Is it okay to think only about what we want, especially if someone else might be hurt, or do we need to think about how what we do affects other people? Well, why don't you read the story and then decide for yourself?

* This passage is from the Book of Numbers 16:22.
**Shimon bar Yochai's midrash appeared in *Vayikra Rabbah* 4:6.

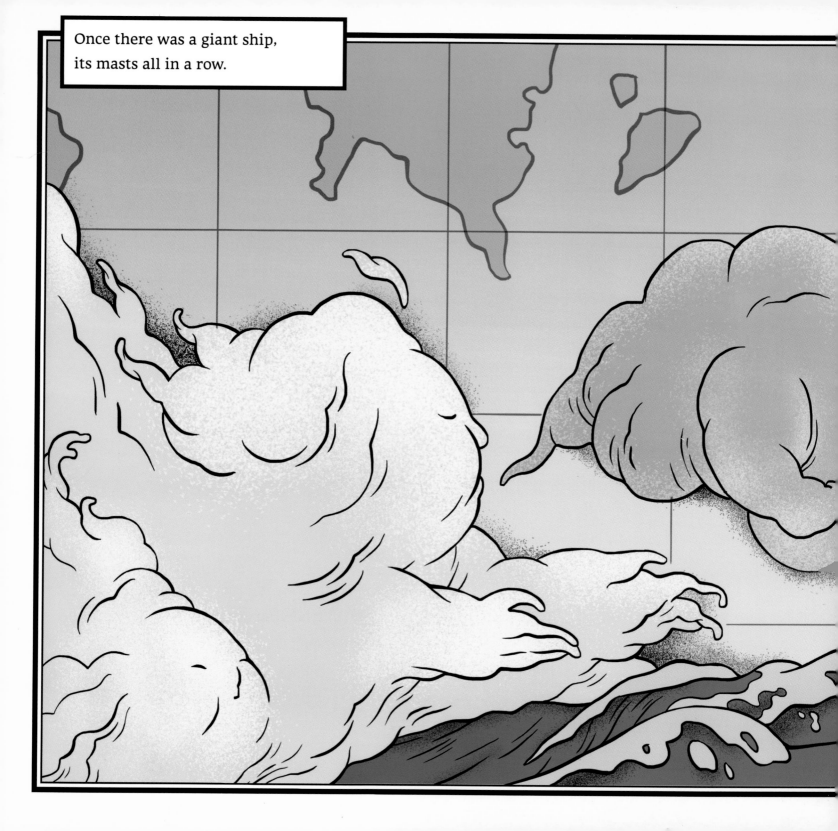

It sailed the seas for seven days,
through cold and rain and snow.

And every sailor had a job:
the first cooked for his mates;

the second steered the mighty ship;
the third unloaded crates.

The fourth man stood upon the deck and swabbed up every crumb;

the fifth man was completely bald; the sixth man liked his rum.

The seventh was a fisherman;
the eighth, a fighter brave;

the ninth, a captain; and the tenth –
a pirate and a knave.

And when the sun begins to set
    into the ocean deep,
then everything is quiet,
    and the sailors go to sleep.

Each sailor has a little room
    no bigger than a nook,
with window, bed, and clean pajamas
    hanging from a hook.

Now, listen to what happened
on a bright and cloudless day,
to all the merry seamen
as they sailed upon their way.

The sea was calm, as smooth as glass,
the morning warm and grand,
when suddenly the captain cried,
"By George, I've spotted land!"

The sailors ten were overjoyed,
and shouted out, "Hooray!
We must prepare for our new home.
We'll be there any day!"

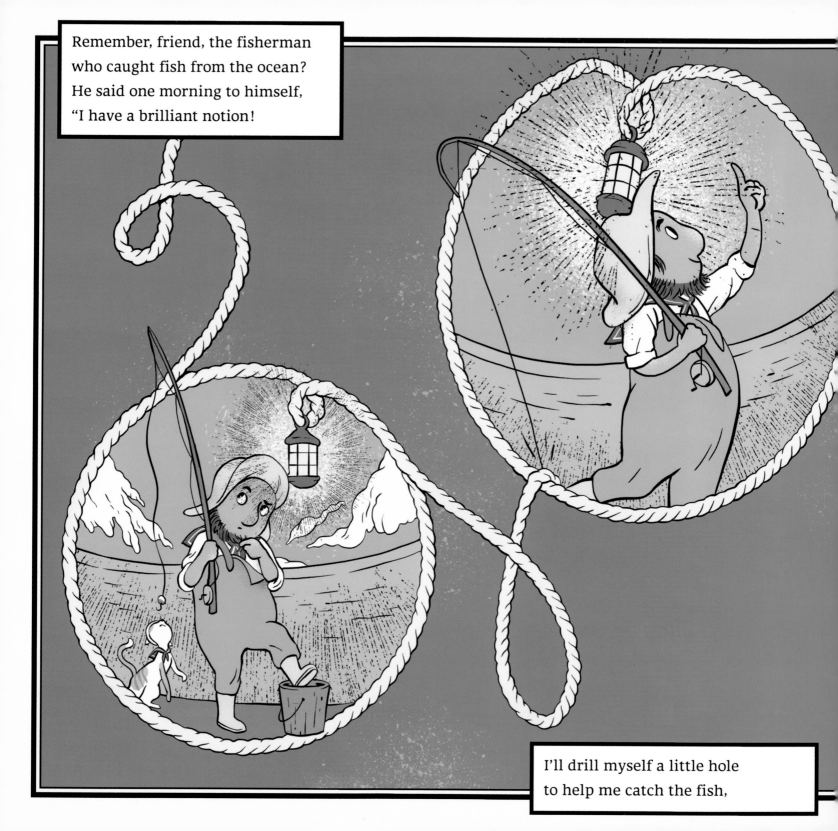

and from my little bedroom
catch as many as I wish!

The fish will swim right up to me,
and I will reel them in.
And when we get to solid ground
my business will begin.

"My heart is singing out with joy
       at my ingenious plan,
for once I open up my shop
       I'll be a wealthy man!"

He went inside his little room
       to drill himself a hole,
then sat down on his wooden chair
       and cast his fishing pole.

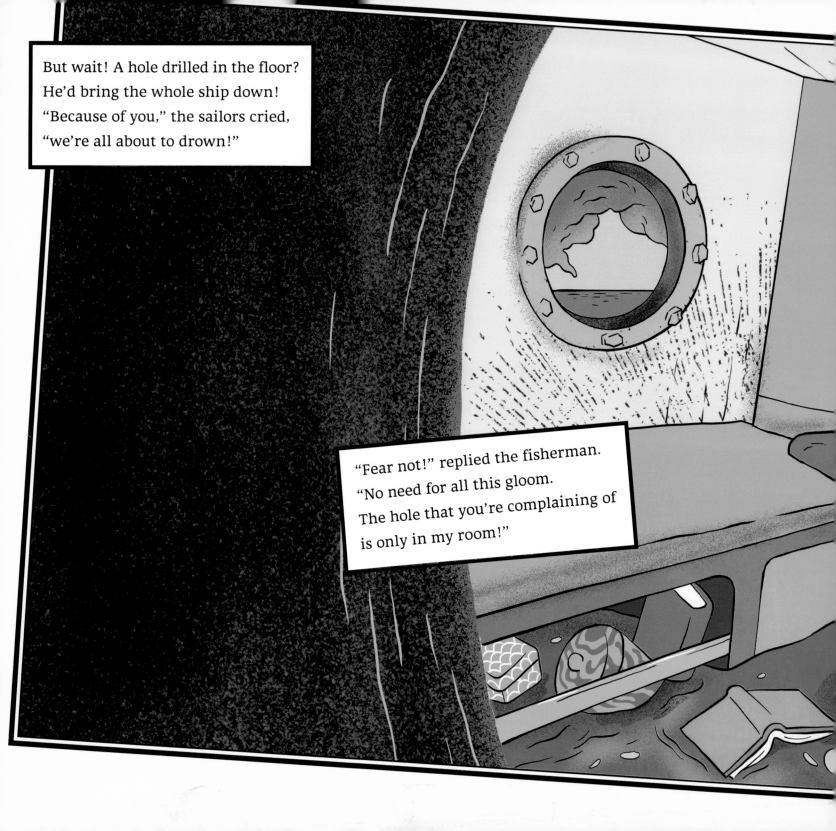

But wait! A hole drilled in the floor?
He'd bring the whole ship down!
"Because of you," the sailors cried,
"we're all about to drown!"

"Fear not!" replied the fisherman.
"No need for all this gloom.
The hole that you're complaining of
is only in my room!"

The fearful sailors bowed their heads
and one began to cry.
"It's true, the hole is in your room,
but all of us will die!"

The sailor's room was flooding fast. How could they stay alive?

They'd have to work together if they wanted to survive.

They filled the hole with mortar so the ship would stay afloat.

Then with mops and rags and buckets they all bailed out the boat.

The fisherman was sorry,
but his mateys? They weren't sore.

"It's all for one and one for all!"
the men began to roar.

The sailors ten were thrilled to see
the shoreline close at hand.
They broke out in a joyful song
as they approached the land.

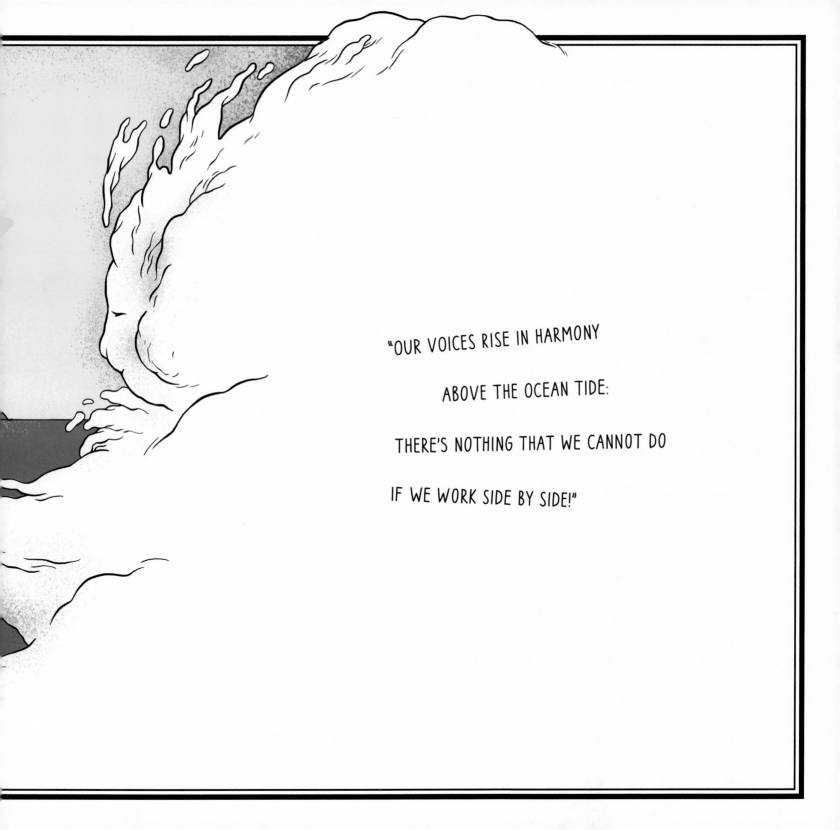

"OUR VOICES RISE IN HARMONY

ABOVE THE OCEAN TIDE:

THERE'S NOTHING THAT WE CANNOT DO

IF WE WORK SIDE BY SIDE!"